Contents

INTRODUCTION

Ghana, country of western Africa, situated on the coast of the Gulf of Guinea. Although relatively small in area and population, Ghana is one of the leading countries of Africa, partly because of its considerable natural wealth and partly because it was the first black African country south of the Sahara to achieve independence from colonial rule.

In addition to being known for its lush forests, diverse animal life, and miles of sandy beaches along a picturesque coast, Ghana is also celebrated for its rich history—its habitation possibly dating from 10,000 BCE—and as a fascinating repository of cultural heritage. The country takes it name from the great medieval trading empire that was located northwest of the modern-day state until its demise in the 13th century. Direct sea trade with Europe, established in the 15th century, had much impact on the area's inhabitants, many of whom actively traded with the Portuguese, Dutch, British, and other Europeans. Forts and castles, many of which still dot the Ghanaian coast today, were constructed by Europeans to protect their trade interests. Although trading was originally centred on the gold that was readily available in the area (and from which the future British colony the Gold Coast would take its name), the focus shifted to the lucrative slave trade in the 17th century. The area later became known for growing cacao, the source of cocoa beans. Introduced there in the late 19th century, cacao continues to provide an important export for Ghana.

Modern-day Ghana, which gained its independence on March 6, 1957, consists primarily of the former Gold Coast. The colony's drive for independence was led by nationalist and Pan-African leader Kwame Nkrumah, who viewed Ghana's sovereignty as being important not only for the Ghanaian people but for all of Africa, saying "Our independence is meaningless unless it is linked up with the total liberation of the African continent." Indeed, more than 30 other African countries, spurred by Ghana's example, followed suit and declared their own independence within the next decade.

Nkrumah quickly laid the groundwork for fiscal independence within the new country as well, embarking on many economic development projects. Unfortunately, decades of corruption, mismanagement, and military rule stymied growth and achievement. By the 1990s, though, the country's state of affairs began showing signs of improvement, and Ghana is now held up as an example of successful economic recovery and political reform in Africa.

Overview

Ghana is on course to meet the global targets for under-five overweight, under-five stunting, and under-five wasting, but is off course to meet the targets for all other indicators analysed with adequate data.

Although it performs well against other developing countries, Ghana still experiences a malnutrition burden among its under-five population. As of 2014, the national prevalence of under-five overweight is 2.6%, which has increased slightly from 2.5% in 2011. The national prevalence of under-five stunting is 18.8%, which is less than the developing country average of 25%. Ghana's under-five wasting prevalence of 4.7% is also less than the developing country average of 8.9%.

In Ghana, 52.1% of infants under 6 months are exclusively breastfed, this is well above the Western Africa average of 32.5%. Ghana's 2015 low birth weight prevalence of 14.2% has decreased slightly from 16.1% in 2000.

Ghana's adult population also face a malnutrition burden. 46.4% of women of reproductive age have anaemia, and 6.6% of adult women have diabetes, compared to 6.4% of men. Meanwhile, 16.6% of women and 4.5% of men have obesity.

CHAPTER ONE

Location, Geography & Climate

Much of the attraction of Ghana is based upon its legacy as the center of the gold, ivory, and slave trade during the 17th and 18th centuries, when the mighty Ashanti empire held sway here. However, Ghana also possesses one of the best game reserves in West Africa, a multitude of good beaches, and plenty of hospitality.

Ghana is one of the five African nations along the northern coastline of the Gulf of Guinea. It is bordered on the west by Cote d'Ivoire, on the north by Burkina Faso, and on the east by Togo. The country consists mostly of low-lying savannah regions, with a central belt of forest.

Ghana's distinguishing geographic feature is the Volta River, on which was built the Akosombo dam in 1964. The damming of the Volta created the enormous Lake Volta, which occupies a sizeable portion of Ghana's southeastern territory.

Lake Volta is also the site of Kujani National Park, though Ghana's best-known park is Mole, located in the north. Unfortunately, neither Lake Volta nor the river itself have yet been developed for touring--although lake cruises are offered, the great majority of water traffic consists of cargo ships.

Rainfall is fairly heavy, particularly from April through September.

History & People

Ghana's rich history centers on the once-great Ashanti empire, which rose to power during the late 17th century and continued to prosper as a center of the 18th century slave trade. The Ashanti capital, Kumasi, was during this period one of the finest and most advanced cities in Africa, and the Ashanti state even employed significant numbers of Europeans as advisors and administrators.

The European presence in Ghana is also marked by the multitude of colonial forts that dot its coastline--strongholds that anchored the European trade in gold, ivory, and slaves. Although Ghana, then known as the Gold Coast, was largely considered a British territory by the latter half of the 19th century, it wasn't until 1900 that the British succeeded in defeating the Ashanti and the area's other strong kingdoms.

Traditional Ghanaian Dishes You Need To Try

There's a lot to learn from a group of people by the way they put together their meals. The ingredients, cooking methods and energy they apply into feeding themselves extend beyond nourishment, with their culinary skills reflecting different beliefs, traditions and habits. As such, experiencing and experimenting with local traditional foods provides an education of the culture, too.

Traditional Ghanaian food is typified by the distribution of food crops. With the prominence of tropical produce like corn, beans, millet, plantains and cassava, most ethnic groups creatively employ these foodstuffs to make mouth-watering dishes for their nourishment. Below are some dishes to introduce you to the scope of local Ghanaian food.

Jollof rice

Originally from Senegal, Jollof is a pot dish of rice prepared with tomato sauce and served with meat or fish that stirs up plenty of interesting debate online. The rice soaks up the juicy flavours and turns orange when cooking, and is a national favourite that can be found in most restaurants or dished out by street vendors at affordable prices.

Waakye

Waakye is another food that exhibits Ghanaians' creative use of rice. The recipe is a medley of beans and rice and was originally a Northern dish, but it can now be found almost everywhere on the streets of Accra. Eating Waakye will open the door to a range of Ghanaian tastes and flavours as the main dish is served with other sides such as fried plantain, garri (grated cassava), spaghetti and avocado.

Banku and tilapia

When you see fish being grilled on the streets of Accra it is most likely to be tilapia, a delicacy among Ghanaians, who spice then grill the succulent freshwater fish. It complements banku, a Southern mix of fermented corn and cassava dough, and very hot pepper, diced tomatoes and onions. Banku is one of the main dishes of the people who live by the Ghanaian coast.

Red-red

Red-red is a filling traditional dish that consists of cowpea beans boiled to make a broth, served with palm oil and soft, fried plantains. It is one of the Ghanaian dishes that doesn't use a lot of spice because the main taste comes from the ingredients it's served with – it can also be dished up with garri to make it even more hearty. Red-red is also a perfect choice for vegetarians as no animal products are used.

Fufu and goat light soup

In the Eastern and Ashanti regions of Ghana, one meal guaranteed to work its wonder is fufu and goat light soup, the proud dish of the Akan. Fufu is a staple food across West Africa but in Ghana, it is made by pounding a mixture of boiled cassava and plantains into a soft sticky paste to go along with aromatic and spicy tomato soup. Fufu can also be found in Northern Ghana, although it is made with yam in this region.

Tuo Zaafi

Northern Ghanaian food is dominated by the use of grains, herbs and meat as these are the main food products of the area. Tuo Zaafi is similar to banku, although it is quite soft and less sticky, and is made by cooking corn dough and adding a little cassava. What distinguishes Tuo Zaafi and makes it a popular meal nationwide is the nutritious and rare herbs used in making the accompanying soup, including dawadawa and ayoyo leaves.

Kenkey and fried fish

Kenkey is another corn-based staple similar to banku, that is made by moulding fermented corn dough into balls and wrapping them around drying corn leaves, which are then boiled. The meal is served with hot pepper sauce, fried crabs, octopus or fish and is a delicacy of the Accran people.

Kelewele

No list of traditional Ghanaian foods would be complete without this savoury side dish. Kelewele is an instant favourite among anyone who tries it, even those who aren't big fans of peppery food. Usually sold as a snack or side dish all over Accra, it is made by frying soft plantains that have been soaked in a medley of peppers, ginger and garlic. The aroma is crisp and strong, while the pleasant plantain adds some sweetness to the sour.

Omo tuo

Omo Tuo (or rice balls) are another traditional Ghanaian food that shows how the population often reinvents the myriad ways of eating rice. It comprises soft boiled grains that are moulded into balls and served with a variety of soups, and makes a great accompaniment to many dishes like fufu.

One present feature in local Ghanaian food is the use of a variety of leaf vegetables and local herbs and spices. The highly nutritious Kontomire stew is made from boiled tender cocoyam leaves, salted fish and boiled eggs, and goes perfectly with boiled yams, plantains and avocado.

CHAPTER TWO

GHANA COOKBOOK

Taco Seasoning I

Ingredients

1 tablespoon chili powder

¼ teaspoon garlic powder

¼ teaspoon onion powder

¼ teaspoon crushed red pepper flakes

¼ teaspoon dried oregano

½ teaspoon paprika

1 ½ teaspoons ground cumin

1 teaspoon sea salt

1 teaspoon black pepper

Directions

Step 1

In a small bowl, mix together chili powder, garlic powder, onion powder, red pepper flakes, oregano, paprika, cumin, salt and pepper. Store in an airtight container.

Guacamole

Ingredients

3 avocados - peeled, pitted, and mashed

1 lime, juiced

1 teaspoon salt

½ cup diced onion

3 tablespoons chopped fresh cilantro

2 roma (plum) tomatoes, diced

1 teaspoon minced garlic

1 pinch ground cayenne pepper (optional)

Directions

Step 1

In a medium bowl, mash together the avocados, lime juice, and salt. Mix in onion, cilantro, tomatoes, and garlic. Stir in cayenne pepper. Refrigerate 1 hour for best flavor, or serve immediately.

Garlic Prime Rib

Ingredients

1 (10 pound) prime rib roast

10 cloves garlic, minced

2 tablespoons olive oil

2 teaspoons salt

2 teaspoons ground black pepper

2 teaspoons dried thyme

Directions

Step 1

Place the roast in a roasting pan with the fatty side up. In a small bowl, mix together the garlic, olive oil, salt, pepper and thyme. Spread the mixture over the fatty layer of the roast, and let the roast sit out until it is at room temperature, no longer than 1 hour.

Step 2

Preheat the oven to 500 degrees F (260 degrees C).

Step 3

Bake the roast for 20 minutes in the preheated oven, then reduce the temperature to 325 degrees F (165 degrees C), and continue roasting for an additional 60 to 75 minutes. The internal temperature of the roast should be at 135 degrees F (57 degrees C) for medium rare.

Step 4

Allow the roast to rest for 10 or 15 minutes before carving so the meat can retain its juices.

Rosemary Roasted Turkey

Ingredients

¾ cup olive oil

3 tablespoons minced garlic

2 tablespoons chopped fresh rosemary

1 tablespoon chopped fresh basil

1 tablespoon Italian seasoning

1 teaspoon ground black pepper

salt to taste

1 (12 pound) whole turkey

Directions

Step 1

Preheat oven to 325 degrees F (165 degrees C).

Step 2

In a small bowl, mix the olive oil, garlic, rosemary, basil, Italian seasoning, black pepper and salt. Set aside.

Step 3

Wash the turkey inside and out; pat dry. Remove any large fat deposits. Loosen the skin from the breast. This is done by slowly working your fingers between the breast and the skin. Work it loose to the end of the drumstick, being careful not to tear the skin.

Step 4

Using your hand, spread a generous amount of the rosemary mixture under the breast skin and down the thigh and leg. Rub the remainder of the rosemary mixture over the outside of the breast. Use toothpicks to seal skin over any exposed breast meat.

Step 5

Place the turkey on a rack in a roasting pan. Add about 1/4 inch of water to the bottom of the pan. Roast in the preheated oven 3 to 4 hours, or until the internal temperature of the bird reaches 180 degrees F (80 degrees C).

Marinated Grilled Shrimp

Ingredient

3 cloves garlic, minced

⅓ cup olive oil

¼ cup tomato sauce

2 tablespoons red wine vinegar

2 tablespoons chopped fresh basil

½ teaspoon salt

¼ teaspoon cayenne pepper

2 pounds fresh shrimp, peeled and deveined

6 eaches skewers

Directions

Step 1

In a large bowl, stir together the garlic, olive oil, tomato sauce, and red wine vinegar. Season with basil, salt, and cayenne pepper. Add shrimp to the bowl, and stir until evenly coated. Cover, and refrigerate for 30 minutes to 1 hour, stirring once or twice.

Preheat the oven to 375 degrees F (190 degrees C). Combine the salt, pepper and garlic powder in a small cup. Place the roast on a rack in a roasting pan so that the fatty side is up and the rib side is on the bottom. Rub the seasoning onto the roast.

Step 3

Roast for 1 hour in the preheated oven. Turn the oven off and leave the roast inside. Do not open the door. Leave it in there for 3 hours. 30 to 40 minutes before serving, turn the oven back on at 375 degrees F (190 degrees C) to reheat the roast. The internal temperature should be at least 145 degrees F (62 degrees C). Remove from the oven and let rest for 10 minutes before carving into servings.

Spinach and Feta Pita Bake

Ingredients

1 (6 ounce) tub sun-dried tomato pesto

6 (6 inch) whole wheat pita breads

2 roma (plum) tomatoes, chopped

1 bunch spinach, rinsed and chopped

4 fresh mushrooms, sliced

½ cup crumbled feta cheese

2 tablespoons grated Parmesan cheese

Step 2

Preheat grill for medium heat. Thread shrimp onto skewers, piercing once near the tail and once near the head. Discard marinade.

Step 3

Lightly oil grill grate. Cook shrimp on preheated grill for 2 to 3 minutes per side, or until opaque.

Foolproof Rib Roast

Ingredient

1 (5 pound) standing beef rib roast

2 teaspoons salt

1 teaspoon ground black pepper

1 teaspoon garlic powder

Directions

Step 1

Allow roast to stand at room temperature for at least 1 hour.

Step 2

3 tablespoons olive oil

ground black pepper to taste

<u>Directions</u>

Step 1

Preheat the oven to 350 degrees F (175 degrees C).

Step 2

Spread tomato pesto onto one side of each pita bread and place them pesto-side up on a baking sheet. Top pitas with tomatoes, spinach, mushrooms, feta cheese, and Parmesan cheese; drizzle with olive oil and season with pepper.

Step 3

Bake in the preheated oven until pita breads are crisp, about 12 minutes. Cut pitas into quarters.

Juicy Roasted Chicken

Ingredients

1 (3 pound) whole chicken, giblets removed

1 teaspoon salt and black pepper to taste

1 tablespoon onion powder, or to taste

½ cup margarine, divided

1 stalk celery, leaves removed

Directions

Step 1

Preheat oven to 350 degrees F (175 degrees C).

Step 2

Place chicken in a roasting pan, and season generously inside and out with salt and pepper. Sprinkle inside and out with onion powder. Place 3 tablespoons margarine in the chicken cavity. Arrange dollops of the remaining margarine around the chicken's exterior. Cut the celery into 3 or 4 pieces, and place in the chicken cavity.

Step 3

Bake uncovered 1 hour and 15 minutes in the preheated oven, to a minimum internal temperature of 180 degrees F (82 degrees C). Remove from heat, and baste with melted margarine and drippings. Cover with aluminum foil, and allow to rest about 30 minutes before serving.

Simple Roasted Butternut Squash

Ingredients

1 butternut squash - peeled, seeded, and cut into 1-inch cubes

2 tablespoons olive oil

2 cloves garlic, minced

salt and ground black pepper to taste

Directions

Step 1

Preheat oven to 400 degrees F (200 degrees C).

Step 2

Toss butternut squash with olive oil and garlic in a large bowl. Season with salt and black pepper. Arrange coated squash on a baking sheet.

Step 3

Roast in the preheated oven until squash is tender and lightly browned, 25 to 30 minutes.

Roast Sticky Chicken-Rotisserie Style

Ingredients

4 teaspoons salt

2 teaspoons paprika

1 teaspoon onion powder

1 teaspoon dried thyme

1 teaspoon white pepper

½ teaspoon cayenne pepper

½ teaspoon black pepper

½ teaspoon garlic powder

2 onions, quartered

2 (4 pound) whole chickens

Directions

Step 1

In a small bowl, mix together salt, paprika, onion powder, thyme, white pepper, black pepper, cayenne pepper, and garlic powder. Remove and discard giblets from chicken. Rinse chicken cavity, and pat dry with paper towel. Rub each chicken inside and out with spice mixture. Place 1 onion into the cavity of each chicken. Place chickens in a resealable bag or double wrap with plastic wrap. Refrigerate overnight, or at least 4 to 6 hours.

Step 2

Preheat oven to 250 degrees F (120 degrees C).

Step 3

Place chickens in a roasting pan. Bake uncovered for 5 hours, to a minimum internal temperature of 180 degrees F (85 degrees C). Let the chickens stand for 10 minutes before carving.

Whole Chicken Slow Cooker

Ingredient

4 teaspoons salt, or to taste

2 teaspoons paprika

1 teaspoon cayenne pepper

1 teaspoon onion powder

1 teaspoon ground thyme

1 teaspoon ground white pepper

½ teaspoon garlic powder

½ teaspoon ground black pepper

1 whole whole chicken

Directions

Step 1

Mix salt, paprika, cayenne pepper, onion powder, thyme, white pepper, garlic powder, and black pepper together in a small bowl.

Step 2

Rub seasoning mixture over the entire chicken to evenly season. Put rubbed chicken into a large resealable plastic bag; refrigerate 8 hours to overnight.

Step 3

Remove chicken from bag and cook in slow cooker on Low until no longer pink at the bone and the juices run clear, 4 to 8 hours. An instant-read thermometer inserted into the thickest part of the thigh, near the bone should read 165 degrees F (74 degrees C).

Insalata Caprese II

Ingredients

4 large ripe tomatoes, sliced 1/4 inch thick

1 pound fresh mozzarella cheese, sliced 1/4 inch thick

⅓ cup fresh basil leaves

3 tablespoons extra virgin olive oil

½ teaspoon fine sea salt to taste

1 pinch freshly ground black pepper to taste

Directions

Step 1

On a large platter, alternate and overlap the tomato slices, mozzarella cheese slices, and basil leaves. Drizzle with olive oil. Season with sea salt and pepper.

Cajun Spice Mix

Ingredients

2 teaspoons salt

2 teaspoons garlic powder

2 ½ teaspoons paprika

1 teaspoon ground black pepper

1 teaspoon onion powder

1 teaspoon cayenne pepper

1 ¼ teaspoons dried oregano

1 ¼ teaspoons dried thyme

½ teaspoon red pepper flakes (optional)

Directions

Step 1

Stir together salt, garlic powder, paprika, black pepper, onion powder, cayenne pepper, oregano, thyme, and red pepper flakes until evenly blended. Store in an airtight container.

Grilled Asparagus

Ingredients

1 pound fresh asparagus spears, trimmed

1 tablespoon olive oil

salt and pepper to taste

Directions

Step 1

Preheat grill for high heat.

Step 2

Lightly coat the asparagus spears with olive oil. Season with salt and pepper to taste.

Step 3

Grill over high heat for 2 to 3 minutes, or to desired tenderness.

Pico de Gallo

Ingredients

6 roma (plum) tomatoes, diced

½ red onion, minced

3 tablespoons chopped fresh cilantro

½ jalapeno pepper, seeded and minced

½ lime, juiced

1 clove garlic, minced

1 pinch garlic powder

1 pinch ground cumin, or to taste

1 pinch salt and ground black pepper to taste

Directions

 Step 1

Stir the tomatoes, onion, cilantro, jalapeno pepper, lime juice, garlic, garlic powder, cumin, salt, and pepper together in a bowl. Refrigerate at least 3 hours before serving.

Roasted Asparagus Prosciutto and Egg

<u>Ingredients</u>

1 bunch fresh asparagus, trimmed

1 tablespoon extra-virgin olive oil

1 tablespoon olive oil

2 ounces minced prosciutto

ground black pepper

1 teaspoon distilled white vinegar

1 pinch salt

4 eggs

½ lemon, zested and juiced

1 pinch ground black pepper

Directions

Step 1

Preheat oven to 425 degrees F (220 degrees C). Place asparagus in a baking dish and drizzle with 1 tablespoon extra-virgin olive oil.

Step 2

Heat 1 tablespoon olive oil in a skillet over medium-low heat. Add prosciutto; cook, stirring, until golden and rendered, 3 to 4 minutes. Sprinkle prosciutto and oil over asparagus. Season with black pepper and toss to coat. Roast in the preheated oven for 10 minutes. Toss and return to oven until firm yet tender to the bite, 5 minutes.

Step 3

Fill a large saucepan with 2 to 3 inches of water and bring to a boil over high heat. Reduce heat to medium-low, pour in vinegar and pinch of salt. Crack an egg into a bowl then gently slip the egg into the water. Repeat with remaining eggs. Poach eggs until whites are firm and yolks have thickened but are not hard, 4 to 6 minutes. Remove eggs from water with a slotted spoon, dab on a kitchen towel to remove excess water, then transfer to a warm plate.

Step 4

Drizzle asparagus with lemon juice. Transfer asparagus to plates, top with poached egg and pinch of lemon zest. Season with black pepper and serve.

Easy Herb Roasted Turkey

Ingredients

1 (12 pound) whole turkey

¾ cup olive oil

2 tablespoons garlic powder

2 teaspoons dried basil

1 teaspoon ground sage

1 teaspoon salt

½ teaspoon black pepper

2 cups water

Directions

Step 1

Preheat oven to 325 degrees F (165 degrees C). Clean turkey (discard giblets and organs), and place in a roasting pan with a lid.

Step 2

In a small bowl, combine olive oil, garlic powder, dried basil, ground sage, salt, and black pepper. Using a basting brush, apply the mixture to the outside of the uncooked turkey. Pour water into the bottom of the roasting pan, and cover.

Step 3

Bake for 3 to 3 1/2 hours, or until the internal temperature of the thickest part of the thigh measures 180 degrees F (82 degrees C). Remove bird from oven, and allow to stand for about 30 minutes before carving.

Roasted Okra

Ingredients

18 eaches fresh okra pods, sliced 1/3 inch thick

1 tablespoon olive oil

2 teaspoons kosher salt, or to taste

2 teaspoons black pepper, or to taste

Directions

Step 1

Preheat an oven to 425 degrees F (220 degrees C).

Step 2

Arrange the okra slices in one layer on a foil lined cookie sheet. Drizzle with olive oil and sprinkle with salt and pepper. Bake in the preheated oven for 10 to 15 minutes.

Ken's Perfect Hard Boiled Egg (And I Mean Perfect)

Ingredients

1 tablespoon salt

¼ cup distilled white vinegar

6 cups water

8 eggs

Directions

Step 1

Combine the salt, vinegar, and water in a large pot, and bring to a boil over high heat. Add the eggs one at a time, being careful not to crack them. Reduce the heat to a gentle boil, and cook for 14 minutes.

Step 2

Once the eggs have cooked, remove them from the hot water, and place into a container of ice water or cold, running water. Cool completely, about 15 minutes. Store in the refrigerator up to 1 week.

Marinara Sauce Yet

Ingredients

2 (14.5 ounce) cans stewed tomatoes

1 (6 ounce) can tomato paste

4 tablespoons chopped fresh parsley

1 clove garlic, minced

1 teaspoon dried oregano

1 teaspoon salt

¼ teaspoon ground black pepper

6 tablespoons olive oil

⅓ cup finely diced onion

½ cup white wine

Directions

Step 1

In a food processor place Italian tomatoes, tomato paste, chopped parsley, minced garlic, oregano, salt, and pepper. Blend until smooth.

Step 2

In a large skillet over medium heat saute the finely chopped onion in olive oil for 2 minutes. Add the blended tomato sauce and white wine.

Step 3

Simmer for 30 minutes, stirring occasionally.

Quick List of Fat Burning Foods in the Ghanaian Diet

A lot of people try to starve their nutrition in a bid to reduce fat. This approach can have negative effects on your body and is not a wise or healthy way to reduce fat. The right way to reduce fats is to eat foods that reduce the possibility of further fat deposition or foods that assist in burning fats, while also taking up calorie-burning exercises like the resistance or weight training exercises. These are exercises that burn fat (both belly and body fat) for up to 48 hours even after you have stopped exercising.

I'm talking about exercises that help your body burn fat even while you are sleeping, resting or cooking. Awesome, right?

So here's a quick list of some easily available fat burning foods in Ghana:

Citrus Fruits

I would rank these as the best fat burning foods around. Eating a breakfast of citrus fruits, or other Vitamin C rich fruits, is one the best ways to start reducing the fat profile of your body. Citrus fruits provide the body with easy energy to hike up its metabolism while also supplying a rich amount of Vitamin C which is scientifically known to help burn fat as it's a vital chemical used by the body in the process of fat metabolism.

Some citrus fruits you can try are Oranges, Grape fruit, Tangerines, Lemon and Fresh Lime. While fruits like Strawberries, Apples, Tomatoes, Grapes, Cherries etc are also good sources of vitamin C.

Depending on your budget, and fruit availability, try to use a mix of these fruits for your breakfast to combine health with taste. You can also try out a "citrus fruit only" breakfast for a few weeks to see how effectively it helps in burning fat around your waist and hips. I've personally seen excellent results with this method of eating a fruit only breakfast.

Fruits in general are excellent foods for fat reduction because they are natural, they are rich in vitamins & minerals, high in water content and low on calories compared to refined foods. Fruits are known to improve body metabolism and reduce bad cholesterol. Paw-paw, bananas, mangoes etc are excellent snack foods as well as breakfast foods.

Oats

The benefit of eating cereals like Oats is that they contain a huge proportion of their calorie profile in terms of insoluble fiber. This insoluble fiber not only gives you a feeling of satiation and thus keeps you from feeling hungry for a long time but also does not contribute to any calorie addition to the body. In fact, any foods that contain a good amount of insoluble fiber would help you in the process of reducing the fat profile of the body.

Vegetables

Except for certain calorie rich vegetables like potatoes, sweet potatoes or yams, most other vegetables have a low calorie profile while containing essential minerals and vitamin that improve the metabolism of the body. When you eat potatoes, if possible, cook them with their skin on because their skin is a good source of insoluble fiber.

Veggies like spinach, pumpkin leaves, water leaves, beans, peas, cabbage and carrots are excellent sources of minerals while being low on calories. Veggies don't contain fats either and their carbohydrate count is very low (even compared to fruits). Cucumbers are excellent as a salad food, low on calories and rich in water content.

The best way to cook veggies would be to boil them or stir fry them with healthy oils like olive oil or coconut oil.

Poultry

If you are a non-vegetarian it would be a good option to eat more poultry than red meats. Poultry like chicken are low on fats and carbohydrates and have a high protein profile. Proteins are not only more complex to digest & assimilate (and thus require a higher expenditure of energy) but they also require more energy to be stored as fats.

Go in for lean cuts and avoid eating the skin of the poultry as it contains a lot of fat. Red meats, or white meats, from lamb, beef or pork, can be consumed in moderate quantities a few times a week, instead of eating them regularly in your diet, because they have a high fat profile (but these meat are a good source of minerals and proteins that can assist in the over-all health of the body when consumed in moderation).

Eggs

An average adult can consume one or two eggs a day (whole eggs with yolk) and obtain necessary protein and minerals from it while also keep a low calorie profile. Infact you can eat as much as 5-6 egg whites and 1 whole egg and this has no effect on your cholesterol levels.

Research show that eggs do NOT contribute to increasing your bad cholesterol profile but can serve to improve your good cholesterol (necessary for a healthy body) when eaten in moderation.

Almonds and walnuts

These are excellent snack foods and can help you feel satiated with just a fistful of these nuts. These nuts are a great source of healthy fats. It has been seen that people who don't consume healthy fats are more likely to gain weight than people who do. This is the reason why it s NOT good to eliminate healthy fats from your diet in a bid to reduce weight.

Fish

Fish is a good source of protein and healthy fats (rich in omega-3, omega-6 fatty acids), and makes for a great lunch or dinner meal. Salmon, mackerel, trout and tuna are not only tasty but are excellent sources of omega-3 fatty acids while also being low on calories and saturated fat content.

Though water would not count as a food, because it has no calories, it would need to mentioned that water helps improve the over-all metabolism of the body and thus helps burn fat. And of course, water helps flush out toxins and thus improves the capacity of the body to stay healthy. Certain foods are rich in their water content and thus help in the process of fat reduction (also foods rich in water content make you feel satiated quickly), some examples are water melons, cucumbers, paw-paw etc.

The benefit of eating these water rich foods is that they supply minerals (electrolytes) along with water and hence do not cause "water intoxication" which can results from drinking too much water while not balancing out the minerals (especially during work outs).

CONCLUSION

Whole foods are better than refined or processed foods when it comes to reducing the fat profile of the body. If there is a choice between a processed foods (like pastries, pizza, chin-chin, small chops, pasta etc) and whole foods (like milk, eggs, chicken, vegetables and